CONVERTED BY LOVE

Anthony "Marsman" Brown

WESTBOW
PRESS®
A DIVISION OF THOMAS NELSON
& ZONDERVAN

Scripture taken from the King James Version of the Bible

WestBow Press books may be ordered through
booksellers or by contacting:

WestBow Press
A Division of Thomas Nelson & Zondervan
1663 Liberty Drive
Bloomington, IN 47403
www.westbowpress.com
1 (866) 928-1240

Because of the dynamic nature of the Internet, any web addresses or
links contained in this book may have changed since publication and
may no longer be valid. The views expressed in this work are solely those
of the author and do not necessarily reflect the views of the publisher,
and the publisher hereby disclaims any responsibility for them.

Any people depicted in stock imagery provided by Thinkstock are models,
and such images are being used for illustrative purposes only.
Certain stock imagery © Thinkstock.

ISBN: 978-1-5127-7730-7 (sc)

Print information available on the last page.

WestBow Press rev. date: 03/06/2017

CONTENTS

CHAPTER 1

BLUE AND ZIBA HIGH SCHOOL YEARS

Love is the greatest thing anyone can experience. It builds you up and strengthens the mind, which controls the whole body. It gives you a steady heart beat and ignites every atom of energy in your body. But there can be a serious backfire if not careful because even though it makes you feel so good -especially in a relationship sometimes, when you think it's the best it can be someone else's distress. Some people wrongfully think love can be sold, others think it can be bought while some people wait all their lives for love to come along but it never happened to them. Falling in love is something that can happen in the strangest ways and places and sometimes you'll be surprised to see the type of person and places that love is forthcoming. It can cause jealousy and a serious grudge in the mind of others but once you find that true love in another human being you should praise God and cherish it.

This is a love story which started out as normal friends

in two different High Schools in two different countries between two eighth grade students who were surfing the web and miraculously met while they were online. The boy's name is Blue who was 14 years old at the time, a Jamaican living in Ontario, Canada. The girl's name is Ziba who was 13 years old at the time, an Iranian living in Iran.

While both of them were surfing the web at the same time from their locations in different countries they stumbled upon each other. Blue was the first to greet her by saying, "Hi what is your location?" Ziba hesitated first before she answered, then she said, "I'm in Iran." "What!" said Blue who was surprised to hear her location because he thought she was in the United States of America then he gave his location in return by telling her that he was in Ontario, Canada. Both of them were very reluctant in giving out more information about each other because they were not sure if the other was telling the truth. In today's world parents teach their children to be very careful when surfing the web because a lot of strange predators come on the internet daily and pretend to be what they are not so they decided to skype each other the following day where they could see each other which was a very good idea. They both agreed to a particular time because the time difference could be tricky, being in different countries.

The next day when Blue Skyped Ziba it took a little while before they got through to each other and finally they could now see each other. When Blue saw her he said, "Hi," she listened carefully to the sound of his voice to make sure that it was the same person before she answered, "Hi, what is your name?" "My name is Blue and what is yours?" asked Blue. She replied and said her name was Ziba which means "beautiful" and she was 13 years old then she asked, "How old are you?" "I am 14 years old," answered Blue. They started to talk more about school work and realized that they both had something in common, they were straight A students at their High Schools. Ziba was not very fluent in the English language but the more they spoke, the more he understood her and appreciated her because she was very intelligent and pretty.

While Ziba was talking to Blue she heard music playing in the background so she asked him, "Is that Reggae music I am hearing in the background?" "Yes, is it played in your country?" asked Blue. "Of course, I listen to reggae music all the time and my father also loves the music," said Ziba. "Wow! That's a real surprise do you go to parties?" "Only if it's a birthday party but most of them are too old fashion you don't hear the music you want to hear," said Ziba. "Tell me more, what kind of sports do you play?" asked Blue. "As a girl, apart from physical education at my school I don't partake in any sports but I love tennis. What sports do you play?" asked Ziba. "I play mostly basketball and soccer but I love soccer the most because I've been playing it since I was a little kid in Jamaica. That's where I'm originally from." said Blue. He told her that if she was in Ontario, Canada she could come and watch him play when he is representing his High School and she would get to love the game. "One other question I want to ask, as a straight A student like myself what books do you love to read?" asked Ziba. "Apart from the Holy Bible and school books I like reading sports magazines which keeps me informed with sporting activity around the world. What do you like to read?" said Blue. "Apart from school books I like reading fashion magazines but that as far as it will go because in my country I will never be able to dress fashionably like the girls in the western world," replied Ziba. Blue told her that on weekends when there is no school he sometimes goes to the movie with his friends or fishing with his dad and she said that she helps her mother around the house on a weekend especially giving a bath to their family pet which is a German shepherd dog. "Lucky for you, the only pet I'm allowed to keep is an aquarium with some fish, I've asked my dad several times for a dog and the answer is always no." said Blue. "It looks like you are always having fun on a weekend I really would love to go out and explore more but only the boys are given that privilege." said Ziba. "You don't even have a hobby like playing video games or friends that you can spend some time with?" asked Blue. "No the only things I do for fun is what I told you before but it's Ok I'll soon be old enough to do as I please." said Ziba. "I understand not having many friends because I always remember something my dad told me last year that two things will determine my future while growing up and the first one is how well I serve God and the other is the type of friends I associate with," said Blue. "My dad is always telling me to be careful because friends will get me into trouble," said Ziba.

They skyped each other every day at the same time except on Fridays and Sundays which they agreed those days were special days. Fridays was Ziba's strict day of worship. She was from a strong Muslim background and Sundays was Blue's strict day of worship because he was from a strong Christian background. They developed a mutual understanding to keep their religion a secret because her dad who is a businessman and from generations of strong Muslims would not allow her to be friendly with a Christian and with Blue parents there would be a big doubt.

One day when they skyped each other they started to gain more confidence while speaking to each other and they started to open up and talk about things that happened in their lives. Blue started telling Ziba about a fight he got into at school that he couldn't avoid. He told her that he was made captain of the junior soccer team because of his superior grades but it didn't go down well with another player. He was also from the Caribbean and thought that he was the best player on the team so he should be captain instead of Blue. Blue told Ziba that one day he was in the changing room and the jealous player started to call him nicknames but Blue didn't pay any attention to him because he always remembered what his father told him about the peace that Christ Jesus the Messiah stood for. This name calling went on for days until one day when they were alone the jealous player punched at him and missed and tried to throw some more punches, so Blue was now forced to defend himself. Blue told Ziba that they were both taken to the Principal who investigated the matter and got to the bottom of it. Both of their parents had an appointment with the principal the next morning in his office and Blue was told that he should have reported the matter from it just got started because things could have gotten out of hand. In the principal office in front of everyone the jealous player apologized and accepted all the blame. Blue forgave him and they became good friends with Blue still being the captain of the team. "Yes I agree with the principal you should have reported the matter from the beginning because you're the leader of the team and straight A students are not supposed to get into fights," said Ziba. "I wanted to keep the unity of the team by dealing with it myself and not reporting anyone but I can tell you that I definitely learned from that experience," said Blue. "I can't remember ever getting into any fights at school or anywhere I think sometimes it's because of my father who is a highly respected man in our district," said Ziba. "I don't want you to even think of anything like that you're too nice for that," said Blue. Ziba smiled and said, "Thank you very much for the compliment."

The next day when they skyped each other Ziba was looking very sad so when Blue saw her sad look he said, "What's the matter why are you looking so down come on talk to me." Ziba started talking to Blue about something that was weighing heavily on her mind and the older she got was the more it was affecting her, she told him that when she becomes 18 years old she have to marry her father's best friend's son who she had never met. She said the marriage was arranged by their parents since she was one week old and her father's best friend son was two years old at the time then she asked Blue, "Does that happened in your country?" "No way! My country is a free democratic country and it's when you grow up you make that decision for yourself," replied Blue. "I wish that was the same here because I feel like some sort of property," said Ziba. "People in my country according to what I understand fall in love first then they get married and live happily ever after. It might sound like a fairy tale ending but it's true, you are masters of your own destiny," said Blue. When he answered her, Ziba sounded very sad because she did not want to get into that type of marriage but in her country it's a tradition which she is bound to keep. Then Blue asked her, "Although you and your arranged husband have never met, do you know anything at all about him or have you heard anything about how he feels about it?" Ziba said, "No I do not know anything at all about him or know anything about how he feels but It's the norm because it was the same with my parents, they were promised to each other from they were three years old and never met until the day of the wedding when they were both 20 years old and they are still together. Lucky for my mom my dad was very handsome, caring and healthy but he hates Christians and if my arranged husband is even sick and not able to carry out his marriage vows I will have to live with it all my life and try to be happy." "I can feel the sadness through the look on your face and the tone of your voice. Can't you run away when you are 18 years old to get away from it all?" asked Blue. "That would be dangerous and a form of disrespect which would bring shame on my family," said Ziba. "I am really sorry to hear that but I can promise you that if you ever need a true friend you can depend on you have that in me," said Blue.

The following night Blue could hardly sleep because he did a research on the internet and saw where a lot of women who found themselves in similar situation like Ziba committed suicide because they just couldn't go through with it. Blue now seeing the real picture was starting to feel the pain and sadness that Ziba felt because they were now good friends and was praying that Ziba would not get depressed and think about committing suicide. This was a situation that Ziba could do nothing about and the older she got was the more it was going to affect her. She was definitely going to need someone to talk to about it and only told Blue because she confided in him so he had to be the one to comfort her in the situation. The following day when they Skyped each other Ziba was still feeling very sad so in order to alleviate the painful situation both of them got pen and paper and wrote down an oath together to be friends for life regardless of the situation.

OATH OF FRIENDSHIP FOR LIFE

Even though we are so many miles apart and not knowing each other very long it feels like we have been friends all our lives or in some other life.

If the rain falls on your roof it will fall on mine too.

If any of us should go on a journey we will never travel alone because we will always travel with each other in our hearts.

If we retire to bed at nights when we dream we will see each other stretching out a helpful hand to assist each other in case we should stumble or fall.

If there's sadness in our lives when the light shines from above it will bring joy and wipe away all unhappiness so we would always be cheerful and never giving up.

If for some reason or other our load is too burdensome to carry we are just a click of a button away from someone who is warm and understanding.

If we should ever find a pot of gold at the end of a rainbow we will share with those who need it most and I'm sure God will bless us.

Both of them signed the paper they wrote on folded it and put it in a safe place where it would be available to them to read when they need comforting.

CHAPTER 2

DEATH OF ARRANGED HUSBAND

The years passed by quickly with Blue and Ziba now in their senior high school year in their countries continued to communicate regularly through Skype. Ziba who was now almost eighteen years old and bitterly trying to forget her arranged marriage which was just around the corner became more loyal to Blue over the years even though they have never met in person and would do anything possible for each other. Up to this point Ziba still had not met her husband to be, but both parents were busily making preparations for the upcoming marriage. Blue and Ziba remained very strong and dedicated students because they never allowed their friendship to interfere with their school work as they remained straight A students and was looking forward to attend College the following year.

One evening when they Skyped each other Ziba had some news which some looked at as sad while for others will not be so sad. Ziba said to Blue, "I have some news which I just got from my dad that my arranged husband died today at the hospital from pneumonia. I sent my condolences to his parents who were looking forward to the marriage and I must inform you that between now and the funeral I cannot communicate with you because of our custom, please understand." Blue told her that he was sorry to hear and he will be looking forward in resuming communication with her soon.

During the next couple of days Blue never left the monitor of his computer waiting for Ziba to contact him because he knew Muslim burial time was short – sometimes as early as the same day. This is the longest period of time since they met that they did not communicate with each other and it was driving him crazy. Blue could hardly eat anything and when he went to bed at nights he could not sleep properly, Ziba was always on his mind. This could go down as the strangest situation in history that someone that he had never met in person could become so much a part of his life. Being a strong Christian he prayed constantly that she would be ok and that soon she would Skype him.

Three days had passed and still no word when Blue's mother looked at him and saw his condition she asked, "Are you Ok Blue? I don't see you going anywhere with your friends. I only see you sitting around looking at the computer monitor with a sad look on your face." He replied, "I'm Ok mom." Later the same day his father noticed his sadness and asked him, "What's wrong Blue are you Ok?" "I'm Ok dad," said Blue. "I have two tickets to the basketball game tonight, you want to come?" asked his dad. Blue replied, "No, I will take a pass tonight." "What! Something is not right with you, you have never refused going to a top basketball game we have to talk," said his dad. Blue started telling his dad everything because that's the type of relationship both of them have. Blue's dad said, "This is a clear situation that you have fallen in love with this girl who is so far away but before too long, once she feels the same way she's going to contact you soon with a good excuse." Blue asked, "Is this how you feel when you fell in love for the first time dad?" "Not really because your mother was my first love and she was never far away" said his dad. Blue asked, "You think I made a mistake in falling in love with someone so far away?" "No I wouldn't say that because she did not say goodbye and from what I've heard, she told you up front that she won't contact you during that period so cheer up and let's go to the basketball game," said his dad. Those words of comfort cheered him up and Blue accepted the invitation to go to the basketball game. One thing he did not tell his father was that she was a Muslim which both he and Ziba kept their religion as a secret from their parents.

On day four there was still no word from Ziba, but Blue remembered the words of comfort from his father and prayed. In the evening after school he went and played soccer with his friends and after the game he and his friends stopped at a soda café. They sat down and spoke about their upcoming prom because it was their final year in high school. Each of Blue's friends already had an idea who they will ask to go with them to the prom but Blue was the only one who wasn't sure and when his best friend Tom asked him, "Who are you planning to ask to go with you?" "The girl I would like to ask doesn't attend our school and she is thousands of miles away," said Blue.

"Wow, she must be really special good luck my friend," said Tom. "Yes she is and thanks," said Blue. When Blue went home he checked the computer monitor for missed call and there was none so he calmly took a shower, did some school work and retired to bed. When Blue was alone to himself lying in his bed he did some thinking and asked himself some questions. What if Ziba's arranged husband had not died? He would have felt a lot worse and things would have really gotten more complicated for both of them because there's nothing any of them could have done. God is good because the whole arrangement was wrong from the beginning and in saying that he was not glad to hear Ziba arranged husband died because he himself was an innocent party to the whole arrangement and maybe he could have felt worse than Ziba about the arrangement. He said his regular nightly prayer and went to sleep.

The next day was day five and Blue came home half an hour later than usual. When he checked his computer monitor for a missed call he saw a written note from his mother at the front of the computer that Ziba called and said she would call back in an hour. Blue almost jumped through the roof of the house the way he was happy that would be about twenty minutes time so he quickly changed his clothes and grabbed a snack then sat before the monitor of the computer to await the call.

Right on the stroke of the hour she called back and when Blue tuned in and saw her he started to throw kisses to the monitor and asked, "How are you Ziba?" She threw back some kisses to him and said, "Fine, I'm Ok." "We must never take this long to communicate again I feel like I've lost some weight and I couldn't stop thinking about you," said Blue. "Me too and I'm now free to marry who ever I want," said a happy Ziba. "Our marriage is a definite must after our college education," said Blue. "Eh that sound like a proposal?" asked Ziba. Both of them laughed and started bringing each other up to date with events that took place when they were off line.

High School graduation was now in the air and all of Blue's school friends now knew for sure who will accompany them to the prom but Blue still was without a prom date and it did not bother him one bit. On the day of graduation Blue who was graduating with straight A's and also being a top sportsperson was the chosen valedictorian. This was like a record for a graduating student with his credentials not having a prom date and being one of the happiest graduates present. Blue parents who were at the graduation saw what was happening but didn't say a word because they fully understood their child.

At the end of the graduating ceremony Blue's parents came prepared and took a number of pictures of the graduating class because this was possibly the last time all his class mates would ever be together like this. Then afterwards it was prom time but Blue went straight home with his parents who congratulated him all the way home. When they reached home Blue saw a brand new car parked in their driveway and asked, "Whose car is that parked in our driveway?" His father parked alongside the car and took out a set of keys and handed it to Blue and said, "Congratulations son! It's yours. This is for your disciplined, hard work and dedication you've shown over the years in school." Blue who had his driver's license went and sat behind the steering wheel of the new car and said, "Thanks mom and dad you're the greatest parents but the journey is not yet finished, College time is just around the corner and I'm going to make you even prouder when I graduate with my pilot licence."

Blue could hardly wait to show off his new car so he started the car and drove it back to where they were keeping the prom. All his school mates were happy to see him but something happened at the prom while he was slow dancing with one of the female graduates which Blue will never forget. His dance partner said to him, "Blue even though you are dancing with me I can feel that the energy is not here your mind is distracted somewhere else but it's Ok." "I'm sorry," said Blue. He now realizes that the only person that he can have that type of fun with and stay focused was Ziba. Everything went well at the prom and they had a good disciplined time that evening.

The next day when Blue skyped Ziba he told her about his new car which he got as a present from his parents. When she heard she jokingly said, "A car, please come and pick me up later and lets run away together because all I want to do right now is to be with you." "I would love that too Ziba but we have to hold on just four more years when we graduate from College before I can do that," said Blue. Blue went on to tell her that her place whether in his heart, his car or in his home is secured and reminded her about their oath of friendship that they signed he will never break it.

CHAPTER 3

BLUE AND ZIBA STARTING COLLEGE

As the weeks rolled by since Blue's High School graduation, it was now time for his freshman year in College and lucky for him he was only about twenty five minute drive to College from his home in his new car. Everything didn't start going well until the second week when he fully settled down because in the first week there was a lot of up and down with things like getting his full schedule and getting to know his way around, he even started to meet a lot of new friends.

It would take Blue four long, dedicated years in college to become a pilot and he was starting to realize that it was a complete 180 from high school. The standard was definitely expected to be a lot higher and he noticed that the lecturers gave tons of assignments and they were very precise about the outcome. Blue realized that time management would be key if he is going to survive and that would definitely include spending less time talking to

Ziba,who had started College in her country for a nursing career.

Blue and Ziba both agreed that Saturdays when they were off from College and worship was the only time when they could communicate. It wasn't an easy decision but they had to remain focused on the long journey ahead.

After about four months in College Blue's father realized that he was only averaging B's instead of A's, which was his regular in high school. So one day his father said, "I hope it's not because of Ziba why your average dropped to B's in College." Blue hesitated before he answered and said, "College life is rough dad but if Ziba was here I could definitely focus more," "I know it is rough because I've been there and done that," said his dad who is a Consultant Engineer. "I love this girl very much, please understand dad I'm doing my best at the moment," said Blue. "I don't want you to feel as if I'm putting any pressure on you because as long as you are doing your best your mother and I are Ok with that," said his dad. "Thanks dad those words of encouragement was definitely what I needed at this time," said Blue. Just as Blue finished making that statement his mother walked into the room and said, "Please continue your conversation don't let because I'm here you're going to be silent." "We were discussing his B average in College because we all know he is an A average student anywhere," said his dad. "What is Ziba's average like in College?" asked Blue's mom. "She is still maintaining her A's," replied Blue. "Oh so she seems to be dealing with this situation a lot better than you are," said mom. "We are all going to sit and talk together on Saturday when Ziba calls you on Skype. I think it's time that we meet her," said dad. "Ok that will be good," said Blue.

The coming Saturday Ziba called right on time and they were all there waiting on the call. Ziba not knowing that Blue's parents were there said, "Hi Blue, how are you? I'm missing you so much," "I missed you too Ziba, I want you to meet my parents they are right here," said Blue who called them to sit in front of the monitor where Ziba could see them. "Hi Mr. and Mrs. Simpson I'm pleased to meet you," said Ziba. "We are pleased to meet you too," said Blue's dad. "How is College Ziba?" asked Blue's mom. "College is great and couldn't be better," said Ziba. "I'm sorry that after all these years we are just getting to know you so we are wishing you all the best and as time go by we can talk and get to know each other more," said mom. "I would love that," said Ziba. "We are going to hand you over back to Blue so good bye for now," said Blue's parents. "Bye Mr. and Mrs. Simpson," said Ziba. Blue's parents left the room to give Blue his privacy and Blue and Ziba chatted for a while until they said good bye to each other.

When Blue finished talking to Ziba and came out to the living room he saw his parents sitting in the sofa waiting on him. "You guys were out here waiting on me weren't you?" asked Blue. "Not really," said his mom while his dad was holding up his hand to give Blue a high five and said, "Wow! She's a beauty queen and sounds very intelligent too, good luck son." "Make sure if you guys should go further with the relationship she must learn to cook Jamaican food because that's the only kind of food you and your father love," said his mom. "Trust me, we are planning to go all the way," said Blue with a big smile.

Every week when Blue is going to Skype Ziba, Blue parents would always remind him to tell Ziba hi for them so one particular day when his mom was out and his father was alone at home he told his father that he would like to have a man to man talk with him. His dad got concerned and asked him, "What is it son, is everything all right?" Blue said, "Yes but there is something I wanted to talk to you about which I should have told you long ago." His father who was reading a newspaper put it aside and said, "Go ahead son." "Ziba parents are very strong Muslims and Ziba herself was raised as a Muslim," said Blue. "What! You know that this is a very unequal yoke situation because we are Christians and the Holy Bible warned against that type of practice?" said dad who put his hand at the back of his head and leaned back in his chair. "I know dad but what am I to do? We love each other," said Blue. "Let's keep this between us for now because if your mother knows she is definitely not going to be pleased. By the way do her parents know that you are a Christian?" asked dad. "No, Ziba kept that as a secret also." said Blue. "Something like that cannot be hidden forever and we have to pray that her dad will take it the same way I took it when he finds out," said dad.

The first year of College rolled by quickly. One afternoon as Blue was driving home from a soccer match; he lost control of his motor vehicle and ran off the road. Lucky for him when he arrived at the hospital and examined by a doctor there was no concussion or broken bones. He was just shaken up but the car was badly damaged. When Blue parents got the news and rushed to the hospital. They saw him lying on a hospital bed resting. The doctor spoke to Blue's parents and told them that he would be Ok but he's going to let him stay in the hospital overnight for observation. The doctor also told them that when he is released the next day he should rest for a few days because he was badly shaken up.

The next day when Blue parents took him home his dad asked him, "What caused the accident son?" Blue said, "I have a photograph of Ziba in the car and I looked at it, the next thing I know I was going down the cliff and then woke up in the hospital." "The love you have for this girl is taking a serious toll on your life, first it was your College grades and now it's your driving." "I'm sorry dad," said Blue. "Don't worry your mother and I are not going to punish you we are just going to do what's best for your own protection, no more driving till you prove to us that you can focus properly," said dad.

In the coming days when he spoke to Ziba he didn't let her know about the accident because he did not want her to worry too much and he was actually Ok. One thing for certain the pain he felt from the accident didn't stop him from expressing his love to her.

Over the years during their communication some of the ways they expressed their love to each other was in the form of songs, gifts and poems which was downloaded from the website. Both of them saw birthdays as God's gift to mankind and Blue's birthday was here again so Ziba wrote him this poem from her heart.

POEM

WHERE DOES THE SUN GO WHEN IT SETS

TO A PLACE WHERE IT NEVER REST

WHERE DOES THE PARTRIDGE GO TO BUILD ITS NEST

TO A QUIET PLACE WHERE THERE'S NO MESS

WHERE DOES THE RIVER GO IN ITS RAPID QUEST

TO THE OPEN ARMS OF THE OCEAN'S CHEST

WHERE DOES THE MOON GO FOR A FULL TEST

TO A GALAXY OF STARS AND NO WHERE ELSE

WHERE DOES MY HEART GO WHEN IT BEATS LONELINESS

TO YOU DARLING, WHO I WON'T SECOND GUESS

HAPPY BIRTHDAY SWEETHEART

"Birthdays should be seen as special to each and every one because we live in a world that gets more and more dangerous every day. We should also be very thankful to the creator for keeping us safe so In this poem I see you as the Ocean and the stars while I hope you think of me as the Partridge, the moon and the river." said Ziba. "A warm thank you from the bottom of my heart and there are no words available to let you know how I truly feel when I read your poem, I love you very much," said Blue. "I love you too sweetheart," replied Ziba.

A few months later Ziba's birthday was here and this was what Blue wrote to her from his heart:

POEM

IN THE HOLY BIBLE BOOK OF PROVERBS (CHAPTER 31 VS 10-31) IT TEACHES ABOUT A VIRTUOUS WOMAN AND THIS IS HOW I SPELT VIRTUOUS IN MY DREAMS, "Z- I- B- A."

Z IS FOR ZERO TOLERANCE (THAT WILL BE OUR APPROACH TO LIFE WHEN WE GRADUATE COLLEGE TO ALL THE OBSTACLES THAT OBSTRUCTS US FROM BEING TOGETHER)

I IS FOR IMPORTANT (THAT'S WHAT YOU ARE TO ME IN EVERY WAY BECAUSE YOU ARE THE PULSATING BEAT OF MY LONELY HEART)

B IS FOR BEAUTIFUL (THAT'S HOW YOU APPEAR TO ME IN EVERY WAY BECAUSE YOUR BEAUTY IS THE ELECTRIFYING RADIANCE OF MY MIND)

A IS FOR AWESOME (THAT'S HOW YOU ARE TO ME IN EVERY WAY BECAUSE YOU MAKE MY DAY IN NO UNCERTAIN WAY.

HAPPY BIRTHDAY ZIBA

Ziba's birthday fell on a Saturday the day when they agreed to communicate with each other and while they were talking Blue said, "I hope you loved my poem which came straight from my heart and the Holy Bible which you said you've never read. I want you to realize that finding words to describe how I feel about you was very difficult." "I loved it and it couldn't be nicer. I hope one day we can read the Bible together," said Ziba.

The following Monday on Ziba's College Campus in Iran she was sitting on a bench under a tree with her best friend whose name was Alaleh. While Alaleh was talking to her, she noticed that Ziba was daydreaming and not answering her. "Ziba!" shouted Alaleh. Ziba responded and said, "I'm sorry, what did you say?" "You definitely didn't hear a word I said, what's the matter? What's on your mind?" replied Alaleh. Ziba started explaining to her about her boyfriend Blue in Canada and how much she misses him. Alaleh responded, "A long distance relationship can be very taxing on the mind and you still have almost three more years to go in College. Why don't you start going to College parties and going on dates with other guys to see what dating them feels like." "Even though Blue is so far away it feels like he is right here with me, I know that I'm not going to enjoy myself with anyone else apart from him," said Ziba. "You have to remember that you were voted as one of the top three hottest girls on campus, every guy would want to go out with you," said Alaleh. "It wouldn't be fair to go anywhere with any of them because they would not get my full attention," said Ziba. "This sounds like Blue is one special superman

I wish you all the best my friend," said Alaleh. "Thanks for the concern," said Ziba and they parted and went in separate direction.

Meanwhile back in Ontario, Canada, Blue was with a young ministry group at his Church when one of the females in the group named Lois, who is a medical student, tried to get his attention. She said, "Hi, why are you so quiet all the time?" "I am not normally a quiet person I'm usually more outgoing but there are certain times when you just have to chill and meditate" said Blue. "I've seen you come to several of these meetings and all you do is just chill," said Lois. "I'm sorry but I didn't know it looked so obvious and the way things are it's going to be that way until I graduate College," said Blue. "You want to talk about it because something is definitely going on," said Lois. "No, I'd rather not because it's a bit personal," said Blue who all that time his mind was on Ziba. "Ok but if you want to talk I'm available" said Lois. "Thanks for the concern," said Blue.

CHAPTER 4

BLUE AND ZIBA GRADUATING COLLEGE

The painful years without each other in person have rolled by and to both Blue and Ziba, it felt like an eternity. Ziba's graduation took place on a Monday and she was awarded a nursing degree while Blue's graduation took place the following Thursday, where he was awarded with his degree and pilot license. He had stepped up the pace to achieve the license in the least possible time.

After their separate graduations both of them sent congratulating messages and pictures of their graduation to each other. After seeing the pictures Blue finally saw what Ziba's father and mother looked like, and right away he was off on the right footing. Blue did not get any sporting award like what he was accustomed to in high school because all his time was taken up in his books. Time was limited and Blue was determined to finish the same time as Ziba so his plan was right on track.

Ziba started working one week after her graduation in one of the local hospitals in Iran and Blue who had several offers from different airlines put off starting to work till three months after his graduation because his plan was to travel to Iran to find Ziba immediately after the graduation. Ziba communicated with Blue that since she graduated and started working, her father had been inviting a number of his wealthy friends to the house and some even having the audacity to ask for her hand in marriage. One day she got fed up and asked her dad "Why are you inviting so many men to the house to harass me, it's bad that I have to put up with it at work with doctors hitting at me constantly, now at home? Give me a break!" He smiled and said, "Ziba, you're a grown woman now and it's time for you to have a husband so I did not see anything wrong with inviting my friends over for a drink of wine." "I see nothing wrong with a drink of wine but they want more than a drink and I want the harassment to stop, please!" said Ziba. "I am sorry that you looked at it that way but I was only trying to help. I will stop," said her dad. "Thank you dad you know that I love and respect you but just give me a little time you will meet my heartbeat soon," said Ziba. He smiled and hugged her and said, "I can hardly wait just make sure he is not an infidel!" Let's hope her father will continue smiling when he finds out that a Christian man had stolen his daughter's heart and that she told him that her heart belongs only to him until the day she dies. After Ziba told Blue what had happened he now knows that he has to act fast. So one day Blue went to his best friend Tom's house to talk to him about his future plans and how he is going to go about them. Both of them were like brothers from as far back as high school so he could confide in him. When Blue sat with Tom he said, "The time is now Tom I'm going to get the love of my life in Iran." "Are you crazy? Iran is a dangerous place for Westerners. Why such a big risk when there are so many beautiful girls here in the West?" said Tom. "All of them put together cannot be compared to Ziba. We have an oath that we wrote together that is unbreakable," said Blue. "Ok if you really feel that strong after so many years she really must be very special to you," said Tom. "You are the only one that knows about it and I've booked my flight and hotel already, I am leaving tomorrow night," said Blue. When Tom realized that he couldn't talk Blue out of it he turned to him and said, "Let me come with you, I wouldn't feel good to know that you went to a dangerous place like that and I'm not there to help you." No Tom it's best if you stay, you look and speak too much like a Westerner you'll be easily recognized. With me I have the right complexion, the accent and I also have a Jamaican passport so I'll get around much easier," said Blue. He told a sad looking Tom goodbye and left.

Early the next morning Tom went to Blue's house when he knew Blue wouldn't be there. He knocked on the door and saw Blue's dad and whispered, "Meet me over by the park, it's very urgent I must talk to you." Blue's dad opened his eyes wide and started to worry when he heard what Tom had to say so he changed his clothes quickly and told his wife that he'd soon be back. When Blue's dad went by the park and saw Tom he had a very sad look on his face so Blue's dad asked him, "Is everything all right? What is it Tom?" "I am sorry I called you away from the house but I didn't want your wife to hear, Blue is leaving for Iran tonight!" "Oh Lord! That's why he has been so quiet for the past few days," said dad "Blue asked me not to say anything but I couldn't sleep last night, I asked him if I could come and he said I will only get in the way. I just couldn't talk him out of it," said Tom. Blue's dad sighed and said, "This definitely has to stay between both of us, if his mother knows she is going to take it very hard and there's nothing I can do because he's a fully grown man with a rewarding profession." Tom said with tears in his eyes, "Going to that country as a Westerner is like trying to commit suicide, I'm not sure Blue fully realizes what he will be up against." "Ziba and Blue have been online lovers for years and it seems as if he has now reached the stage where he is feeling scarred and severely wounded if she is not with him. The only thing possible we can do is pray to the Most High God in Christ Jesus the Messiah for his protection," said dad. "Have you ever met her or should I say have you ever seen her because I've never seen her?" asked Tom. "She is marvelous, she's a beauty queen." said dad. "Now I understand why Blue has been turning down all these girls for so many years, let's hope that everything goes well and I can be a best man at a wedding" said Tom. Blue's dad wanted to laugh but he couldn't because he knew that an even bigger problem was on the horizon which he didn't say to Tom, she was a Muslim and her dad doesn't know that he's Christian. He told Tom thanks for telling him and in the next few days he will be fasting and praying.

Blue's dad was determined that he wouldn't let his son go to Iran without saying goodbye because there's a possibility that he may not come back alive so he called the airport and found out what time the flight to Iran was leaving. When dad got the time he went to the airport four hours before the schedule flight and waited for Blue to arrive at the airport just to see him. After about two hours waiting he saw Blue arriving in a taxi and when Blue stepped out of the cab and was heading to the check in area he called to him. When Blue looked and saw that it was his dad he asked, "How did you find out? I couldn't tell you and mom because you would have worried and may become sick." "Tom and I spoke and we decided to keep it as a secret from your mom because she's the one who would have been devastated. Here's some money to take with you," said his dad. When Blue took the money he said, "Thanks I'm glad you understand because after so many years of communicating I must go and I'm confident that my faith in Christ Jesus the Messiah will keep me safe." His father hugged him and said, "Go and catch the plane son and bring back my future daughter in law!" "Goodbye dad," said Blue and they parted.

CHAPTER 5

BLUE LANDING IN IRAN

After a long flight the plane was finally landing in Iran's International airport and capital city of Tehran, when Blue checked the time the clock in the airport was showing midday. Blue dressed in his red, green and gold tam, the reggae king Tee Shirt with belt to match had an easy access going through customs with his small New Testament Bible hidden at his ankle in his socks. His luggage was a bag over his shoulder because he only took with him what he would need and when he approached a smiling female custom officer and gave her his Jamaican passport she said, "Welcome to Iran!" "Thank you very much for such a warm welcome," Blue said. "You're Jamaican?" she asked. "Yeah man." Blue said. "How long will you be staying?" she asked. "About a month," Blue replied. With no hesitation he was granted the amount of time he needed and was on his way through the airport. There was no doubt that his accent and Jamaican passport did the trick for him but he noticed that security was everywhere so he calmly went along his merry ways without anybody asking him any more questions.

When he reached outside of the airport he chartered a taxi and asked the driver to take him to the hotel where he had his booking. This particular hotel was carefully chosen because Ziba told him that it was the best hotel which was closest to where she lived. It was a bumpy ride in the taxi cab which took about thirty minutes to arrive at the hotel and from what he had seen it was a very beautiful hotel. He paid the taxi driver who knew very little English and went inside the hotel where he checked in. Blue was so tired from the long flight that he had a shower and went to lie down in the bed and got some rest.

After resting for about three hours Blue got dressed and went downstairs to the hotel's lobby with a sports magazine which he took with him to read. While he was sitting in the lobby he carefully listened to the other guest to hear if any of them spoke any English. He didn't have any luck until about an hour after when he heard this man who was employed as a door man at the hotel speaking to someone and to his surprise, spoke brilliant English. He didn't look much older than Blue was so he knew it was time for him to make his move. Blue got up and went towards the door and he opened the door for Blue and he politely told him, "Good evening and thank you." He said, "Good evening do you need a cab sir?" I said, "It's Ok, I'm just taking a little walk." To my surprise when he heard Blue accent and looked at him he asked him if he was Jamaican and he said, "Yeah man!" "Is it your first trip here?" he asked. Blue replied "Yes I, you're the first person that I have met here so far that speaks such good English I would really like to speak with you more." He told Blue that he was very busy at the moment because a lot of foot traffic was coming in and out of the hotel and he has to open the door for them so when he's off duty in another hour they could sit and have a drink and talk some more. Blue loved the sound of that so instead of standing around waiting on him he took a little walk around the hotel vicinity just to get to know the place a little more.

While Blue was on his observation walk around the hotel building he noticed a commotion that was taking place on the street beside the hotel. Blue saw some youngsters that appeared to be in their teens burning an American flag with a certain level of intensity on their faces. They were shouting in what appears to be Persian language words that he assumed to be bad. Other people were just moving on minding their own business but Blue stopped for a few minutes and looked because something like that was unusual to him in the Western world where he was from. When they finished burning the American flag the protesters just went on about their business in different directions and that was the end of the protest so Blue just continued his walk. Blue now realizes that he's not watching television but is seeing the real issues of Iran everyday life live and direct.

Blue returned to the hotel's lobby in about an hour time and the door man was there waiting so Blue said to him, "I hope you weren't waiting long because I came back the time when you said I should." He said, "It's Ok I'm here every day anyhow my name is Pete." Blue said, "My name is Blue from Kingston, Jamaica." "Come there's a bar across the street we can go over there and have a drink and talk," said Pete. While they were on their way to the bar Blue asked Pete about the protest he saw and

Pete told him that it's the norm it happens every now and again when they can get their hands on an American flag and he shouldn't pay it any mind.

When they reached the bar and sat down Blue asked Pete while making an order for both of them, "Where did you learn to speak English so fluently?" Pete said, "I was born in England and lived there till I was ten years old, unfortunately my English father died and my mother who is an Iranian decided to come back to Iran because there was too much discrimination." "Oh come on discrimination is everywhere," said Blue. "I agree but while you can change everything else you can't change your skin color, discrimination is the type of sin that affects your generation and deprives you of your dignity," said Pete. "Don't worry I know exactly what you mean," said Blue. "I want you to know that I go a long way with Jamaicans because my grandfather was a member of Marcus Garvey UNIA movement way back and he used to tell me a lot about it before he died when I was five years old. I also noticed that most of the elder folks here know about Marcus Garvey's work quite well. On the other hand I'm also a big supporter of Reggae music which is a big hit with the younger folks," said Pete. "How is life here in Iran and have you ever felt like going back to the land of your birth?" asked Blue. "No, even though my father side of family is English the thought had never come to me I am living here approximately twenty years now and life so far has been good to me," said Pete. "When a man travels this far it's either business or woman. Why have you travelled so far to be in Iran?" asked Pete. The more they spoke was the more he started to trust and have confidence in Pete because he had to trust somebody if he's going to go further. Blue explained and told Pete everything except that he's a Christian and while Pete was sitting and listening he smiled and said, "I understand because Iranian women are some of the most beautiful women in the world and very disciplined too." "I'm glad you understand" said Blue.

Blue showed Pete the address and asked him, "When can you take me to this address and how far is it away from here?" "It is about ninety minutes, I will try to borrow my wife's car in another two days when it's my day off and take you but you're going to have to buy petrol," said Pete. "It's Ok no problem," said Blue.

Meanwhile back in Canada at Blue's parent's home, Blue's dad was sitting in the living room with a very worried look on his face when Blue mom walked in and saw the look on his face. She asked, "Is everything Ok, why are you looking so worried?" Blue's dad shook his head from left to right without saying a word so she got suspicious and asked, "Is Blue Ok? Because this is the longest period that I've not seen or heard from him since he was born." "Honey sit down let me talk to you because regardless of the situation you should know. Your son has gone to Iran," said dad. "What! How long did you know about this?" asked Blue's mom. "The only person he told was Tom and Tom told me when he couldn't convince him not to go. I went to the airport and saw him before he boarded the plane and gave him some money so that while there he wouldn't fall short," said dad. Blue mother started to cry and had to be consoled by dad. She said, "How could he be going to do such a dangerous move and not say goodbye. This is like trying to commit suicide!" "He begged me not to tell you because he knew you would take it badly but we have to remember that he is now a fully grown man with his profession so all we can do in a situation like this is pray. He doesn't need our permission to go" said dad. "What is so special about this girl that he would travel thousands of miles across the world to risk his neck?" asked mom. "You have to be a man to understand that," said dad.

CHAPTER 6

BLUE SURPRIZES ZIBA

It's now day three with Blue waking up to the rising sun shining on him through his open window. If everything goes well he should finally meet Ziba today. It was Thursday morning at 10 o'clock the day when Ziba said she was always off from work so he had to grab something to eat and start preparing himself because Pete would be coming to pick him up at 12 o'clock which is two hours away.

At approximately midday Blue went downstairs to the hotel's lobby fully dressed to impress in a black vest with a picture of the reggae king with his guitar on the front of the vest. He sat in the hotel lobby and waited for Pete who didn't arrive until about fifteen minutes after. When Pete saw Blue he said, "Are you all set and ready to meet the love of your life?" Blue smiled and said, "Just get me there let me swoop her off her feet." "Yeah man," said Pete who answered like a Jamaican.

They started the ninety minutes journey and along the way they stopped at a petrol station to purchase gasoline. "Fill her up," said Pete in Persian language to the gas station attendant who was his friend. When the gas station attendant looked in the car and saw Blue dressed in the reggae king vest he said, "Reggae, one love!" Unfortunately that was the only English he knew so Blue just used his fist to knock the attendant's fist and said, "One love!" They started the journey again in dry and dusty condition and along the way Blue saw several anti-American slogans painted on walls. He didn't say anything to Pete about them he just ignored them as they got nearer to their destination. When they were about five minutes away Blue asked Pete to stop at a flower shop that he could buy a red rose because his first meeting with Ziba in person he had to impress. They stopped at the flower shop and Blue got out of the car and bought a beautiful red rose which was fresh and well scented. This stop was the most impressive so far because all the young folks in the vicinity when they saw the reggae king vest he had on started shouting, "One love!" Blue just waved back to them and said, "One love!"

They finally reached their destination and Pete parked the car and showed him the house and said, "Go and see her and take your own time because I'm in no haste, I'll wait in the car." "Thank you for your patience my friend," said Blue. He alighted from the car feeling very nervous walked up to the door and knocked. When the door opened Ziba's mother opened the door because he remembered her face from the graduation pictures and he said, "Good evening can I speak to Ziba Please." She said, "Good evening, wait." She turned around and went inside to call her. Blue could hear Ziba footsteps coming to the door and with every footsteps she made his heart skipped a beat, his knees were weakening but he had to be strong and with a blink of an eye she was out of his dreams standing in front of him. When Ziba looked at him with her eyes wide open as if she was in a state of shock, Blue looked at her and said, "Hi Ziba." She stood silent for a few seconds experiencing a loss for words then she shouted, "Blue!" They hugged each other for about five minutes none of them wanted to let go with tears of joy coming from her eyes and she said, "Blue you are finally here." "I had to come I couldn't go on living without you," said Blue and gave her the red rose he bought. "Thanks come inside," she said. When Blue went inside Ziba introduced him to her little brother Omeed and parents who looked amazed when they saw how their daughter greeted this young man. "Good evening Mr. and Mrs. Ahmadi," said Blue and shook their hands. "Ziba, is this the gentleman who you told me about? The airline pilot I remember," said her dad. "Yes dad," said Ziba. Her dad who was now about to launch a friendly attack turned to Blue and asked, "Young man which Mosque do you worship in your country?" Ziba immediately stepped in to protect Blue before he could give an answer and said, "Daddy please we can all talk about that at another time." "I just wanted to know who my daughter's heart had gone to that's all," said Ziba's dad.

After telling Mr. and Mrs. Ahmadi goodbye Ziba took Blue to a beautiful nearby park and on their way to the park Ziba said, "I can't believe we are finally together after so many years of being in each other heart." "It's good to see you and you're even prettier in person," said Blue. Ziba smiled and said, "Thanks and you're so tall and handsome. This is where we're going to sit and talk every time you come to see me and do all our planning on how we are going to deal with the situation. We have more privacy here when you come and I want you to know no matter what my heart belongs only to you till death." "Mine too and if you want to you can come by the hotel sometime," said Blue. "I can't let anyone see me going in or coming out of your hotel room and we are not married that's too much risk," said Ziba. "I'm sorry you explained to me before I just forgot, I really want to kiss your lips so bad Ziba," said Blue. "Me too, be patient the time will come when we can do anything," said Ziba.

They sat in the park hugging and talking to each other for almost an hour about his long journey to Iran but now he was there he couldn't care less about the obstacles he had to clear. Blue said to Ziba while hugging her, "Ziba I love you very much and if it wasn't the love I have for you I would not have come on such a dangerous mission. I was given only one month stay in the country so I hope you will be willing to start packing while I'm here." "It's not as easy as it seems but I love what you just said," replied Ziba. "Did you at least renew your passport?" asked Blue. "Yes I have my travel documents intact," said Ziba. "Good, well at least we are off on a good start," said Blue. "I'm going to have to start talking to my mom about this first before I approach my dad because he's going to want to speak for everyone and there's no way he's going to give the answer we want unless he knows more about you," said Ziba. "You already know everything and it's what you think that counts," said Blue. "He's not going to see it that way but I'm going to have to work on something," said Ziba. "Ok but remember time is short," said Blue.

Time was going quickly so Blue told Ziba that he had to go because someone was waiting on him. He took Ziba and introduced her to Pete who was waiting patiently in the car reading a newspaper. It is the first time Ziba is seeing Pete even though they are both natives of Iran but never the less she accepted him as her friend also because he is Blue's friend. Blue told Ziba goodbye and told her that he will come and see her on Saturday because Friday is Ziba day of worship and when they drove off heading back to the hotel he kept looking back until she was out of sight.

When Blue got back at the hotel he wanted to call his parents in Canada to let them know everything was Ok but he hesitated because he doesn't know the type of intelligence they have in Iran when you are making calls to the West. So to play it safe he had to cool it even though he knew his parents would be worried sick if they don't hear from him soon.

Meanwhile, back at Ziba's house after Blue left her parents asked her a few questions about Blue. Her mom asked, "That handsome young man who came here today seems to be your heartbeat because I've never seen you greet anyone like that before?" asked Ziba mom. "Yes mom he is," answered Ziba. Her father who sat and listened to the conversation between Ziba and her mother said, "No passing grade can be issued from me until I know some more about him because looks can be deceiving," said Ziba's dad. "Remember you gave passing grade to someone that Ziba didn't even know to marry so I don't get it, we have to remember that Ziba is now a grown woman capable of making her own decisions," said her mom. "That was a long standing tradition in Iran which works out better than the Western world because look at the amount of divorce they have over there," said Ziba dad. "Ziba, God has granted you the privilege which I didn't have to choose your own husband and as a bright intelligent girl I know you are whoever you choose is Ok with me," said Ziba's mom. Ziba avoided eye contact with her father because he wasn't pleased with what her mom had said so she did everything to avoid a religious conversation because she knew that could spoil everything.

CHAPTER 7

CONVERSION OF ZIBA

It was now 11 o'clock Saturday morning and Ziba and Blue had arranged to meet at a particular location in the nearby park to her house. Their meeting will be at 4 o'clock this afternoon because she leaves work one hour before at 3 o'clock and lucky for Blue Pete will be off work at 2 o'clock so again he had arranged to take Blue for a particular fee which was more than affordable to him.

At 2 o'clock Blue was prepared and ready so he presented himself in the hotel's lobby to await Pete. This time Blue took with him the small New Testament Bible which he carried in his socks through customs. To be on the safe side Blue wrapped it in a piece of foil paper and again hid it in his socks because the Holy Bible was banned in Ziba's district.

At 2:15pm Pete and Blue started their journey taking the same route having the strings of anti-American slogans. They chatted while travelling but one thing Blue still did not let him know, that he was a Christian, he just didn't trust him that much yet. On their way Pete asked Blue, "Are you planning to marry Ziba one day? Wow, she's awesome." "Most definitely," said Blue. "Then I wish you all the best my friend," said Pete. "Thank you," said Blue.

They arrived at Ziba house five minutes early and Pete parked while Blue walked to the door and knocked. Ziba was the one who answered the knocking of the door because she was expecting him. Blue went inside said hello to her parents and her little brother who he made a little kite for which he made from pieces of bamboo he got from Pete. When Blue gave him the kite he said, "Thanks I love it! Can we go to the park and fly it?" "Sure you can come with us," Blue said. While their parents were sitting in the living room watching television they left the house and walked to their specific location in the park. While Ziba and Blue were sitting on the park bench having their conversation her little brother was running around the park flying his kite so he did not affect their privacy. Blue and Ziba greeted each other with a discipline hug because there were some other people in the park and of course they were avoiding problems. Blue and Ziba started to talk about the journey to and from her home and his stay at the hotel but the main topic was now their future. Blue led that discussion because he wanted to talk about things that have been laid down in the Holy Bible and the Holy Koran. Unfortunately, Ziba had never read the Holy Bible but Blue had done his research on both so she decided to sit back and listen while he did a comparative analysis of Christ Jesus the Messiah and Prophet Mohammed.

Blue took the New Testament Bible from his right ankle sock, wrapped in foil paper so no one could see what they were reading. Ziba laughed at his ingenious method to get around without causing any trouble and they were quite safe because the closest person to them was about thirty yards so no one could see or hear what they were saying. Blue said to Ziba, "A lot of things have been said and done over the years but the way of Christ Jesus the Messiah is never done. I've circled some of Christ Jesus the Messiah's words here in the Bible and folded the pages take it and read them and when you are finished I am going to ask you some questions."

<u>WORDS OF CHRIST THE MESSIAH</u>

(Matthew Chapter 5 vs 44) – But I say unto you, Love your enemies, bless them that curse you, do good to them that hate you and pray for them which despitefully use you, and persecute you.

(Matthew Chapter 5 vs 7) – Blessed are the Merciful, for they will receive Mercy.

(Matthew Chapter 18 vs 21-22) – Then came Peter to Him, and said, Lord, how oft shall my brother sin against me, and I forgive him? Till seven times? Jesus saith unto him, I say not unto thee, Until seven times: but, Until seventy times seven.

(Luke Chapter 6 vs 29 - 30) – And unto him that smiteth thee on the one cheek offer also the other; and him that taketh away thy cloak forbid not to take thy coat also. Give to every man that asketh of thee; and of him that taketh away thy goods ask them not again.

(Matthew Chapter 7 vs 12) – In everything do to others as you would have them do to you. For this is the law and the prophets. (THE GOLDEN RULE)

(Luke Chapter 6 vs 37) – Judge not, and ye shall not be judge; condemn not, and ye shall not be condemned: forgive, and ye shall be forgiven;

(Matthew Chapter 5 vs 9) – Blessed are the peacemakers: for they shall be called the children of God.

(John Chapter 8 vs 7) – So when they continued asking him, he lifted up himself, and said unto them, He that is without sin among you, let him first cast a stone at her. (She was accused of adultery)

(Romans Chapter 12 vs 18) – If it is possible, so far as it depends on you, live peaceably with all men.

After Ziba finished reading the Holy Bible Blue mentioned to her something from the other side of the coin a particular section he read in the Holy Koran (Surah 9 : 5) which was the total opposite of what Christ Jesus the Messiah stood for. That section quoted the direct words of the well love and highly respected Prophet Mohammed that Blue wanted to use to compare with the words of Christ Jesus the Messiah.

* (SURAH 9 : 5) – In this section of the Holy Koran Prophet Mohammed told his followers to ambush and kill non-Muslims.

After Blue finished telling her about Prophet Mohammed's words to his followers in the Holy Koran he asked her, "You have just read the true facts from the first translated English version of the Holy Bible and those are the words of Christ Jesus the Messiah. Does He Christ Jesus the Messiah appear to you like someone who would **SHOOT, BOMB and KILL** anyone or influence anyone to do those acts?" "No Blue," she said with a concerned look on her face. "Well, the ball is in your court and I did not disrespect anyone by mentioning what's in the Holy Koran because those were the words in the Holy Koran. You can do your own research of the Holy Koran and check to see if I'm speaking the truth then do the comparison," said Blue.

Ziba sat down and listened to everything Blue was saying because everything he said was new to her and it was her first time she read anything from the Holy Bible but Blue had one more thing he had to address. He said, "I remember something that you told me a couple of years ago you said that your father told you that Christianity is the white man's religion and his proof of that is a portrait that Michael Angelo painted a few hundred years ago, well let's take a look at the facts in the Holy Bible that have all the answers."

(Revelation Chapter 1 vs 14-15) – His head and hairs were white like wool, as white as snow; and his eyes were as a flame of fire; and his feet like unto fine brass, as if they burned in a furnace; and his voice as the sound of many waters.

When Ziba finished reading Blue said, "This was how the writer saw and described Christ Jesus the Messiah in the Holy Bible. Before we continue I must first let you know that Christianity is for all races, the Holy Bible book of (Romans Chapter 10 vs 12-13) teaches us that there is no difference between any race on earth and color does not matter because whether black or white we are all related in some way or the other but in your case knowing the truth is very important. Does this sound like a white man with blue eyes?" "Most certainly not!" said Ziba. "Well I rest my case I want you to know that Christianity is the only religion that teaches total forgiveness and last but not least, Christ the Messiah is the only one on record that never sinned," said Blue.

"When I leave here today I would really love to leave this Holy Bible with you that you can read and know the miracles that Christ performed especially conquering death and giving Christians hope, things that no one else had never done but it would be too risky I couldn't live with myself if someone found it and something should happen to you," said Blue. "You're right but I will never forget what I just learned" said Ziba. "Ziba any good news yet about coming to Canada with me?" asked Blue. "I spoke to my mom but I didn't tell her that you are a Christian and she said I should be careful because my father would never allow it so we have to work on a different plan," said Ziba. "Whatever decision you make he is going to have to live with it because it's your life and you're not a child. So sleep on it because when we meet again right here we are going to have one because we are two adults and don't need our parent's permission to make decisions," said Blue. "Ok," she said and gave him a tight hug then walked him to the waiting car. When they reached the car Ziba said, "Hi Pete how are you?" "Fine it's good to see you again," said Pete. "Make sure you take good care of him please," said Ziba. "I will, goodbye," said Pete and drove off with Blue looking back at Ziba until she was out of sight.

On their journey back while Blue and Pete were having a conversation Pete asked Blue a surprise question, "You are a Christian aren't you?" Blue who was shocked to hear the question did not want to deny Christ the Messiah answered, "Yes but how did you know?" "The first time I took you to see Ziba you told me that you don't love to work on Sundays and it's only Christians that don't like to work on Sundays so I guessed correctly," said Pete. "I didn't want anyone to know but I opened up to you because I saw you as someone I could trust," said Blue. "You did the right thing when you kept it as a secret because you didn't know anything about me but don't worry you can trust me and I want you to know that a lot of Christians are here in Iran regardless of how the situation is," said Pete. "Thanks very much for understanding because I needed a friend and God sent you," said Blue. "Before we reach the hotel I'm going to stop and let you meet my mother so at least you can know something about me," said Pete.

About twenty minutes after Pete pulled up the car at his mom's gate and said, "Come let's go inside." When they went inside Pete introduced Blue to his mom and said, "Mom this is my friend Blue from Kingston, Jamaica." "I'm pleased to meet you, should I say mam?" said Blue. "You can call me aunt Ana, yes I'm pleased to meet you too I can hear the Jamaican accent. How are

Negril and Dunn's River? Are they still beautiful?" asked aunt Ana. "You know about Negril and Dunn's River?" asked Blue. "Sure Pete's father and I visited Negril and Dunn's River, Jamaica once before Pete was born and they were beautiful places then but the best part of Jamaica was the food the curry goat, the steam fish with okra and the jerk chicken," said aunt Ana. "I didn't know that you went to Jamaica mom," said Pete. "Your father and I have been to a lot of places before he died and Jamaica was one of them a matter of fact your father's mother was Jamaican according to what I can remember and that's all I know about her because she died before your father and I got married," said Pete's mom. "What! That's interesting a piece of me is actually in Jamaica," said Pete. Then Pete's mom turned to Blue and asked, "What brought you to Iran?" Blue explained everything to her the same way he explained it to Pete so she smiled and said, "I wish you all the best and I think you have made a good choice because Iranian women respect and listen to their husbands. That's why the divorce rate here is far lower than the Western world because we don't contradict our husbands which is ungodly so take it from me you'll never regret it. Go after her." "Thanks aunt Ana I'm glad Pete took me here those are good words of encouragement which I'll always remember," said Blue and he told her goodbye and they continued their journey to the hotel.

On their way to the hotel Pete made one more stop which was on the same route and it was getting late so he had to pick up his wife from work because he had the car. When he stopped at her work place she was waiting and Pete said to her, "Thara this is Blue my friend from

Kingston, Jamaica. Blue this is my beloved wife Thara."
"I am pleased to meet you," said Blue who gave up the
front seat of the car to Thara so she could sit beside her
husband. "Oh the car looks very clean today," said Thara.
"I had it washed today," said Pete. While they were driving
Thara said to Blue, "Aren't you missing your nice Jamaican
food Pete's mom told me about," "Very much a matter of
fact I just spoke to aunt Ana," said Blue. "Oh you met,"
said Thara. "She even told us that Pete's grandmother was
Jamaican," said Blue. "What! A part of Pete is Jamaican
and he runs so slow," said Thara. Blue laughed when he
heard her teasing Pete. "What sweet you behind me, you
want a race right now?" asked Pete. "No, no it's Ok," said
Blue. "How did the day go for you guys?" asked Thara.
"Irie and hope it will continue to be like that when we visit
Ziba my heartbeat again," said Blue. Thara laughed and
said, "I wish you all the best my friend." "Thank you," said
Blue as they arrived at the hotel to drop him off.

Meanwhile in Canada by Blue's parent's house Tom
his best friend stopped by to find out if anyone heard from
Blue. When Tom knocked on the door and Blue's dad
opened the door Tom said, "Good day Mr. Simpson, how
are you feeling today?" "Real bad because I've not heard
a word from Blue and his mom is now up in arms," said
Mr. Simpson. "You told her? Wow!" said Tom. "I had to
Blue had never taken this long to communicate with us
no matter where he was and I did not want to lie to her. I
am also experiencing sleepless night so you know I'm very
tired," said Mr. Simpson. "I am also feeling very worried
and the temptation is growing more and more to go to
Iran," said Tom. "It wouldn't make any sense because he

had not told us exactly where he was going and that place is dangerous and big," said Mr. Simpson. "Then what are we going to do? Somebody has to do something!" said Tom. "All we can do right now is trust Christ Jesus the Messiah and pray," said Mr. Simpson.

When Ziba retired to bed that same night she remembered everything she learned from Blue and was so impressed with the words of the Holy Bible that she said these silent words in prayer because she couldn't let anyone hear her saying a Christian prayer.

<u>HER PRAYER</u>

HEAVENLY FATHER IN CHRIST JESUS THE MESSIAH

I'VE WALKED IN DARKNESS ALL MY LIFE

BEING LED BY THE BLIND

DOWN A DEAD END DRIVE

BUT NOW I SEE THE TRUE LIGHT

WHICH I ACCEPT WITH ALL MY HEART

THAT YOU ARE THE TRUE PRINCE OF PEACE

AND THANKS FOR USING BLUE

TO GIVE ME THAT SIGHT

AMEN

CHAPTER 8

BLUE AND ZIBA ARE ARRESTED

The next day which was Sunday Blue did not go and visit Ziba because it was his Sabbath Day so all he did was rest and pray. Later in the said evening after Pete finished working he contacted Blue and told him that he has two tickets to the top of the table Premier League soccer game at the nearby stadium with kick off time at 7 o'clock so he asked Blue if he wanted to go. Blue without hesitation accepted the invitation because as an ardent soccer fan he was curious what a soccer match would be like in Iran. A few hours after about 6 o'clock Pete picked up Blue at the hotel and headed to the soccer stadium.

When they reached the stadium there was ample parking so Pete parked and then both of them joined the long line to get into the stadium. When they got inside there was a lot of people moving around and hustling to get the best seats when a little incident happened. Blue who was not used to the hustle and bustle situation accidentally stepped on a man's foot, "I'm very sorry," said Blue. The man got very upset over the minor incident pushed out the foot Blue stepped on and said, "What are you are you blind or something? Wipe it off!" Blue who had tissue in his back pocket took out a piece bent down and wiped off the man's boot in order to be a peacemaker. But with all of Blue's effort to keep the peace the man was still behaving boisterous and said, "You are lucky I was in a good mood because I would make you pick up some of your teeth next!" Pete who was standing nearby observing the incident stepped up to the man with the front of his vest slightly open so the man and not Blue could see the Desert Eagle pistol in his waist said, "It looks as if you don't like when my friend stepped on your dirty foot a while ago? Fool!" The man seeing the pistol in Pete's waist and hearing Pete cold voice starting to shiver said, "I'm sorry it's Ok I was just joking." "I thought so," said Pete softly that no one else could see or hear him and the man turned and walked away in the opposite direction never to be seen again. "What an awful man," said Blue. "Don't worry he was just trying to throw his weight when he realized you were a foreigner fortunately you don't see occurrences like those often in Iran," said Pete. Both of them went to their seats and stood to the national Anthem which was played by a band just before the start of the game. The game was played quietly in a sportsman like manor without any more disturbances.

On Monday Blue arranged with Pete to take him to visit Ziba again during the time Ziba and Pete would be off from work. As usual he prepared and presented himself with a little gift for Ziba in the hotel's lobby on time and waited for Pete to arrive. Pete arrived about ten minutes late but that was Ok because while he was waiting he saw some Airline pilots dressed in uniform walked into the hotel lobby one of whom he recognized as his class mate while he was at flying school. When Blue saw him he went and greeted him asking, "What's happening Abdulla? What are you doing in this part of the world?" "Excuse me, this part of the world is my home I'm from Saudi Arabia originally and I was only in Canada as a student," said Abdulla. "How are you enjoying the job so far?" asked Blue. "I started last week flying my country's National airline and so far it's Ok," said Abdulla. "I am only here as a visitor and I'm going home soon," said Blue. "What airline are you working for?" asked Abdulla. "I haven't started working as yet but as soon as I get home I will be starting with one of three choices and at the moment I haven't made a final decision as yet," said Blue. "Ok that sounds good, I'm sorry you and I can't talk some more because I just got off and I am going to get some well needed rest to start flying again at midnight," said Abdulla. "You know we pilots can meet up anywhere in the world so until we meet again my friend," said Blue. When they parted Blue signaled to Pete who just walked in that he was ready.

When Pete saw Blue he said in a Jamaican greeting, "What a gwan big man?" Blue smiled and said, "Ever since you heard from your mom that a piece of you was from Jamaica you're trying to walk and speak like a Jamaican." "I'm still learning and I have a lot more to learn, come on let's go my brother" said Pete.

The journey to Ziba's house had started again and as usual on both side of the road the anti-American slogans were clearly visible. Both of them chatted along the way but Pete mentioned that he had something he was concerned about he said, "Blue I see you as a brother which means you're more than a friend but there's something you must clearly understand that when Ziba's father finds out that you are a Christian it might get very dangerous so you and Ziba have to be careful and plan properly." Thanks for your concern my brother I asked Ziba to come with me to Canada, she did not give me a direct answer but she promised she would give me one today," said Blue. "My prayer goes with you and I want you to know that I have your back no matter what. I have two loaded AK47 rifles in the car trunk just in case we have to defend ourselves it's as serious as that. Can you use a gun?" "I have never used one and I don't think I'll ever need to use one because I trust in the one and only true living God Christ Jesus the Messiah who I depend on to guide and protect me and believe me he never fails!" said Blue. "I hear you my brother we're approaching the house now so be prepared to meet the love of your life again and remember there's no rush," said Pete. "Thank you my brother," said Blue.

Blue came out of the car and was walking towards the front door when it just opened without him knocking. Ziba was the one who opened it because she was looking out for him through the window because she was expecting him. When Blue saw her he presented to her his gift and said, "Good evening, how are you feeling today?" "I'm good especially now I see you and thanks for the gift," said Ziba. "Where are your parents?" asked Blue. "Both of them went to the hospital to visit an old friend who is very sick and they took my little brother with them," said

Ziba. "Does that mean we are alone where no one can see us?" asked Blue. "Yes we're finally alone," said Ziba. Both of them stood in front of each other staring into each other's eyes and while they were doing that their faces got closer and closer until their lips finally met. It was magical and they hugged each other so tight that it was as if both of them were floating on a cloud in cyber space. It went on continuously for more than five minutes when Ziba started blowing very hard pulled away and said, "Blue! Although we are both adults in the eyes of man we are children in the eyes of God. I want to just like you but we have to cool it because the next step must be done in the context of marriage." Blue had to sit down before he could answer, "I'm sorry Ziba." "There's nothing to be sorry about I was close to melting point too," said Ziba. "Please can I have a glass of very cold ice water?" said Blue also blowing very hard. Ziba laughed and said, "Sure we were this close in getting into trouble as children of God."

After Blue finished drinking the water and cooled down he looked at Ziba, smiled and said, "After waiting so long this kiss have proven to me how much I love you." "I love you just as much but we must remember that while we can hide from man we cannot hide from God so we have to be careful," said Ziba. "What time are you expecting the return of your parents?" asked Blue. "I'm not sure it all depends on how long they decide to stay, come let's go to the park before the neighbors start to get suspicious that something is going on," said Ziba.

While they were on their way to the park Blue said, "Instead of going to the park why don't we go and have dinner together." "That would be great," said Ziba. "You would have to direct us to the best restaurant around because you know I don't know the area very well," said Blue. "By the way what kind of food do you like?" asked Ziba. "Sea food is my favorite," answered Blue. "What! I don't believe this it's my favorite too no wonder why we take onto each other so much because most things we have in common! Ok let's cross the street and take the next bus it will be a fifteen minutes bus ride from here," said Ziba. They crossed the street and about five minutes after the bus arrived.

When they reached the restaurant Ziba said, "Although I've never been inside I heard that the food is good and this is where most tourist go when they are in the area." "Where ever is Ok with you is Ok with me," said Blue. When they were going inside Blue remembered to be a perfect gentleman by opening the door for Ziba and when they got a table for two he also remembered to pull out her chair. Each kindness Blue showed Ziba said, "Thank you sweetheart." They felt very relaxed and comfortable when they sat down. Ziba had to do the ordering because although the food looked and smelled good Blue didn't understand the names on the menu sheet so she explained to him. Blue said, "I feel so much in oneness with you that whatever you order for yourself order the same for me." She did just that and whatever she ordered it was delicious. While they were there eating and talking to each other Ziba said, "I have been doing some reading on the internet and seen where the biggest celebrated holiday in the West is Christmas. It looks wonderful and I would really love to experience it." "It's my favorite holiday with families coming together celebrating the birth of Christ Jesus the

Messiah and exchanging gifts," said Blue. "I see people doing a lot of shopping during the days before Christmas and everyone was looking so cheerful and happy with some singing Christmas carols," said Ziba. "It's also the season for giving and helping the less fortunate," said Blue. "I can hardly wait to be a part of that," said Ziba. "Ziba once God spare life we are going to live and live happily," said Blue. "Blue let this go down on record as our first official date a day we will never forget," said Ziba. "I agree with that and if God spare life and we should live to celebrate our golden anniversary we must never forget this place, I am going to record the name of this place when I get back to the hotel," said Blue.

While they were on their first date Ziba's parents returned home and before her dad could enter the house the next door neighbor called him aside and told him that Ziba was locked in the house with a man. Her dad was furious and in so doing he went up to her room to look for her. When he didn't see her he checked her bed to see if it was pulled up and checked under the bed to see if anyone was hiding. Everything was intact but because of the magical moment with Blue she forgot to put away her diary and left it on her bed. When her father saw it he took it up and began to read it and what he saw made steam came through his ears. She wrote that Blue convinced her that Christ Jesus the Messiah is the true prince of peace and the only way to salvation.

While there were problems at Ziba's house she was at the restaurant unknowing to her dad. While Ziba and Blue were on their date in a good mood she asked him a question, "If we had gone all the way and had sex at the house would you still love me the same?" "Of course! As I see it our love goes beyond sex, It's the fulfillment of our soul and a heartfelt blessing that will mature through the hands of time which can only be felt when there's trust and understanding that we have," answered Blue. "Even if I had no experience because I'm a virgin Blue?" said Ziba. "I'm a virgin too but in time to come that will change soon for both of us," said Blue. When Ziba and Blue finished making their plans at the restaurant Blue paid the bill and both of them headed back to the house via the bus. When they came off the bus she hugged him and walked him to the car. "Hi Ziba," said Pete. "Thanks for bringing him and please take good care of him," said Ziba. "Good bye Ziba," said Blue and while the car was driving away he looked back the entire time until she was out of sight.

Ziba on her way home started to sing feeling very happy until she opened the door and went inside her house. "Hi mom, hi dad," said Ziba when she saw them. "You're a disgrace! You brought a Christian into my house and blasphemed by converting to Christianity. How could you betray me like this?" said her dad angrily. "What are you talking about dad?" asked Ziba. Dad showed her the diary and said, "This! What you have in this is a testimony of what you are." "How could you violate my privacy like that?" said Ziba. "You know that no unmarried couple is to be alone in any house by themselves. Did you fornicate also?" asked her dad. Ziba's mom stepped in and consoled her when she started to cry. "I see him coming here almost every day as if he lives here. Where does he live?" asked her dad. "I don't know," said Ziba. "If I catch him around here again may Allah have mercy on him!" said her dad and walked out of the house in anger to make a report to the police.

When night came Ziba could hardly sleep because she and Blue didn't have any communication by phone so she knew she must go and warn him. That means instead of going to work in the morning she must take the bus to the hotel and warn him before he comes back to the house. While she was lying in her bed she could hear her father in the living room loudly cursing and issuing threats of what he was going to do when he catches that Christian boy who will never leave Iran alive. And while he was cursing he was cleaning his Beretta pistol which he hadn't used in quite a while. But what her father didn't understand is that once you put your trust in Christ Jesus the Messiah He will guide and protect you and even though Christ Jesus the Messiah teaches love and forgiveness His wrath can be more catastrophic than any human being can imagine.

As the sun begins to rise in the east Ziba is up bright and early and dressed for work. She made sure she had her breakfast because she knew this could be the longest day of her life. Unknowing to Ziba her father arranged for someone to trail her the entire day because he suspects that she was going to meet Blue somewhere and she was the only one who knows where to find him.

She travelled on three different buses until the third one dropped her off right at the hotel bus stop. She walked into the hotel compound and saw Pete working at the front door and said to him, "I didn't know you worked here." "Sure didn't Blue tell you this is quite a surprise seeing you here this morning?" said Pete. "What is Blue room number? Its urgent." said Ziba. Pete showed her the elevator and told her to come off at the fifth floor turn left and look for room #516. When she reached and knocked at the door Blue opened the door and said, "Ziba what a surprise!" They hugged each other tight and while she was hugging him she said with tears in her eyes, "My father found my diary and read it, he knows everything and he's looking for you with the police." "I am not leaving here unless you are coming with me!" said Blue. "I'll come with you because I don't trust him anymore now that he knows that I'm a Christian," said Ziba. "Do you have your passport?" asked Blue. "Yes I came prepared," said Ziba. When Blue started to pack his belongings he paused for a while and took out a small box with an engagement ring inside. He went up to Ziba held her left hand, bent down on one knee while looking in her eyes and said, "I've waited agonizingly for years, travelled thousands of miles and risked my life but still didn't see the right time to do this because of a complicated situation. Well I see nothing stopping me now, Ziba will you marry me?" Ziba looked in his eyes and without hesitation shouted a resounding, "Yes!" He got up off his knee and slid the ring on her finger then he stared in her eyes and saw her glowing beauty which started to mesmerize him. She stared back at him with her shields down and offering no resistance to the love of her life who lifted her up took three steps with her in his arms and laid her on the bed and started to kiss her passionately on the bed. While they were kissing and lost in the passion of their emotions they heard a loud knock at the door. Both heard the knock but tried their best to ignore it when the person knocked again even harder, "Who's there?" asked Blue. "It's the police open the door or we'll break it down!" said the knocker. "It seems as if they had trailed you here," said Blue who had no choice but to get up and open the door quickly. The police came in searched the room and arrested both of them and took them away in handcuffs to jail.

Meanwhile in Canada when Blue's parents went to Church his father went up on the podium and told the Church congregation that Blue had gone to Iran and they had not heard anything from him. He begged the congregation while trying to hold back tears to join him in prayer for the safe return of his son. Everyone in Church knew how dangerous that country was especially for Christians so his request was granted. Other relatives like aunts, uncles and cousins etc. from Jamaica and other parts of the world who heard what had happened also called Mr. and Mrs. Simpson to voice their concerns.

CHAPTER 9

BLUE AND ZIBA SENTENCED

Finding himself in jail wasn't a part of Blue's plan but it's the harsh reality of life that no matter how careful you are things happen that you have no control over. Blue and Ziba were held in separate gender jails awaiting trial for things that he doesn't have a clue what they were talking about. He couldn't see Ziba from where he was held but he could see one of the guards so he asked him, "The woman who was arrested with me is she Ok?" The guard did not understand much English so he told Blue to wait and went for another guard who understood the language. When the other guard came Blue asked him the same question and he said, "She is Ok she is on the other side by the female section." "What are we charged for and when is our court date?" asked Blue. "She is charged for blaspheming while both of you for fornicating and conspiring with a Bible which is banned in her district," said the guard. "What! I thought you have to have sex to fornicate, we didn't have sex," said Blue. "Save you defense for when you face the district council tomorrow," replied the guard. "Can you take me to see my friend?" asked Blue. "No you will see her when you sit side by side before the council tomorrow," said the guard.

Meanwhile at Ziba's house her mom was furious when she got the news of Ziba and Blue's arrest when Ziba's dad walked in through the front door. She said to him, "You mean to tell me that you sent Blue and our daughter to jail because they fell in love and are planning their marriage." "I don't care about Blue but Ziba blasphemed and betrayed me so they got what they deserved," said Ziba's dad. "I can bet if Ziba had accepted the marriage proposal of one of your wealthy friend's, things would have been different" said Ziba's mom. He got silent for a while and then he broke the silence with a question, "You know anything about this boy to be taking up for him like this? How do you know that he's not a spy?" asked Ziba dad. "I am not going to swear for anyone but after him knowing Ziba for so long and then travelling thousands of miles across the world just to be with her, that is what you call true love," replied Ziba's mom. "Once you disrespect Prophet Mohammed it doesn't matter who you are I'm done with her," said Ziba dad. "She'll never forgive you for this so you just lost a daughter and I want you to remember that you and I came together because of a practiced tradition not love. Ziba found that true love and you are trying to take that away from her. What are you going to tell Omeed when he grows up?" said Ziba's mom. "I am not the one who's going to try her, the district council will determine her faith tomorrow," said her dad. "You know that there's a possibility of her getting the death sentence for falling in love with her childhood friend. If that happens I'm done with you too because you're a wicked man and you have to be either brave or stupid to ever eat anything from me again. I just couldn't live with it!" said Ziba's mom and walked out of the room crying.

When Pete their friend came to look for them in the afternoon by the jail with some food the guards allowed him to speak to Ziba first and all she did was cried bitterly and barely muttered some words from her mouth saying, "They won't allow me to see Blue but when you speak to him tell him that I love him till death and I'm praying." "I will see him in a few minutes so you can depend on me to do that," said a very sad Pete. The time was short so they took her back and brought out Blue and immediately Pete gave him Ziba's message. When Blue heard the message he said, "Thanks my brother I feel the same way too but I don't really need any food because between now and the trial tomorrow I'll be fasting and praying." "Don't worry my brother I will be praying too and I won't be far away," said Pete. The guard stood and watched from a position that he could hear everything. The time was up and a sad looking Pete had to leave.

The day of the trial was here and the guards on duty by the jail put Blue in handcuffs and led him to the court room. When he reached the court room Ziba had not yet arrived because she was further away and he was put on a bench to sit down in court. A few minutes after Ziba arrived in handcuffs too but Blue couldn't move when she saw and called to him telling him that she loved him. They sat on separate benches at the front of the packed court room on either side on the court isle with Pete and Ziba's mom present watching the proceedings. The judge came in the court room shortly after and the court was called to order then the trial begun. When the charges were read and Ziba and Blue were asked by the judge, "How do you plead?" "Not guilty," said both of them. Only two witnesses were there to testify and they were her father and the next door neighbor.

The next door neighbor was first to be called to give evidence and he testified that on the given day both Blue and Ziba were locked in the house alone for about an hour and they were unmarried. He said he could not see what they were doing but the district law states that unmarried coupled must not be locked up alone together unless witnesses were there. When he was finished testifying the Judge asked Blue and Ziba if they had any question and while Ziba was crying Blue answered, "Sir we have no question at this time but this is a clear example of what Christ Jesus the Messiah spoke about in the Holy Bible that people will see the speck in another person eyes and not see the plank in theirs." "You said you have no question for the witness so please be quiet," ordered the judge.

After the next door neighbor stepped down Ziba father was next to give evidence and he testified that he read Ziba's diary and saw where she blasphemed by denouncing Prophet Mohammed and converted to Christianity. He said all this was because of her lover who is sitting here in court and he pointed to Blue. When he finished testifying the judge asked them if they had any question and while Ziba was still crying Blue answered, "Yes," and turned to Mr. Ahmadi and asked, "How could you do something like this to your own daughter?" Mr. Ahmadi answered, "It doesn't matter who you are once you disrespect Prophet Mohammed you must pay the penalty." "No further question sir because now I know for certain what I'm up against," said Blue.

When both Ziba and Blue were asked to give their side of the story they individually said the same thing that they did not have sex and a doctor's examination can prove that they were telling the truth. They also said that the only reason why they were at the house alone was because Mr. and Mrs. Ahmadi went to visit a sick friend at the hospital so the fornication charge is unfair. As for the blaspheme charge Blue said he can prove to the court from the Holy Bible and the Holy Koran that Christ Jesus the Messiah is the true Prince of Peace because Prophet Mohammed instigated to his followers that they must ambush and kill all non -Muslims in (Surah 9:5) in the Holy Koran. While Christ Jesus the Messiah placed a lot of emphasis to all believers in the Holy Bible to forgive, love thy neighbor and thy enemies. If Ziba read them both and decided to convert to Christianity why should she be put through this because if a Christian converts to Islam there's no criminal charge by the Christians. Blue words in court caused a lot of muttering in court and the judge had to bang on his desk in order to bring order in the room.

After Blue finished speaking and there were no other witnesses to be called the judge summed up the case and ordered Blue and Ziba to stand so they could hear the verdict of the all Islamic jury. The jury unanimously found them guilty. The judge before giving sentence said that Islamic laws are different from those in the west and they are in Islamic territory so they must pay the consequences. The judge said, "Miss Ziba Ahmadi if you re-tract your statement about Prophet Mohammed you will spend only five years in prison but if you don't you will be stoned to death before the sun goes down while Blue will stand and watch you die. Now you Mr. Blue Simpson will spend five years in prison before you are deported back to your country." The judge left the court room and both Blue and Ziba were led away under tight security.

While Ziba was awaiting her execution she was allowed one visitor because of the death sentence and that was her mother who said to her, "Please Ziba you're young do the right thing and start over again when you will still be young." Ziba looked at her mom and said, "They can only hurt my body but they can't hurt my soul. The Apostles did not back down when they saw the dangers they had to face so why should I?" Ziba mom started to cry when she heard how resolute she was and before long the visiting time was up and Ziba was taken back to her cell.

While in her cell there were three other women in the cell with her all awaiting execution. One of them stabbed her husband to death, the other committed adultery and the other killed a man who tried to rape her but the court did not accept her story. All three women sympathized with Ziba who they thought did nothing and should never be in that situation. The woman who killed her husband looked at Ziba and said, "You have a chance Ziba, why don't you denounce the Christian God and live? If we had your option we would have done it." "I will never denounce Christ Jesus the Messiah the true God of the apostles. The Holy Bible says to die in Christ Jesus the Messiah name is to gain and anyway you take it I would die because I could not survive five years in this undesirable situation," said Ziba. With Ziba strong faith, inner strength and boldness she was able to gain the respect of her cellmates who because of their reputation were feared by the other prisoners on the cell block. Ziba cellmate who committed adultery on hearing the boldness in Ziba speech said to her," "I can't believe that a person awaiting death can be speaking so boldly, you're truly a child of God." Meanwhile Blue in his cell could not communicate with his cell mates because of the language problems.

While Blue sat in his cell he prayed this prayer:

HEAVENLY FATHER IN CHRIST JESUS THE MESSIAH

PLEASE HEAR MY CRY

I PRAY TO YOU FROM MY HEART BECAUSE ONLY YOU UNDERSTAND

WHAT WE TRULY FACE

WE WERE PROSECUTED BECAUSE WE LOVE AND OBEY YOU

I KNOW THAT THEY CAN'T TOUCH US UNLESS YOU ALLOW IT

SO BY THE SWEAT OF OUR BROWS

AND THE BLOOD YOU SHED ON THE CROSS

PLEASE DELIVER US

IN CHRIST JESUS THE MESSIAH PRECIOUS NAME I PRAY

AMEN

It was time of decision Blue and Ziba were led from their cells in shackles under tight security and when they reached the pit Ziba was to be put in to be stoned to death, Blue looked at the guard and said in words of desperation, "Please let us die holding hands together." "We can only do what the court ordered," said the head guard. Blue turned and shouted to Ziba, "No matter what we'll be together always, I love you!" "I love you too Blue," said Ziba.

When Ziba was put in the pit and was asked by the court officer, "This is your last chance to denounce Christ Jesus the Messiah and respect Prophet Mohammed. What do you say?" "I will not denounce Christ Jesus the Messiah, the true God of Paul, Peter, James, John and all the other apostles in the Holy Bible!" replied Ziba who was now ready to die in Christ Jesus the Messiah's name. Just when Ziba was done saying what she was saying Blue cried and started to pray, "Christ Jesus the Messiah if this is your will then please let us come home together!"

The court officer lifted his right hand and was about to give the order for the stoning to start when there was a sudden earthquake which shook the ground hard and caused buildings nearby to start to fall. With no clouds in the sky veins of lightning came down touching the ground which caused panic among the guards and executioners.

This caused everyone present except Blue and Ziba who was unable to move to run for their lives. The speed they ran the Olympic one hundred meter champion would be a joke if he was present. The earth quake and lightning went on for about fifteen minutes and there were serious structural damages all around. When everything subsided the guards came back looking for Blue and Ziba and all they saw were the shackles that were used to hold them prisoners. "Spread out we must find them they can't be far!" said the chief guard who knew that his job would be at stake if they were not found quickly. The second in command guard said to him, "After seeing how we angered the God that they serve you really want us to bring down his wrath again." "You want to try explaining their escape to our superiors," said the chief guard who was determined to recapture them and he didn't knew where they had gone.

Meanwhile back in Ontario, Canada Blue' Mother and father had an appointment with their family doctor with Blue's mother being treated for depression; she just cannot get her mind off Blue who is her only child. Blue's father being treated for insomnia, he just cannot sleep at nights because he is constantly thinking of Blue who is his only child also. While they were waiting to see their doctor Blue mom said to his dad, "I am sorry we didn't have another child because this is the sort of situation that you face when you have only one child." "Please don't think that way because if anything I will be the one to blame, I was too busy working all over the world and not having any time for kids," said dad. "It's not fair to take the blame because I was equally guilty, I had a rough pregnancy with Blue so I was very afraid to get pregnant again," said mom. "We have to continue to pray that everything is Ok and leave it in the hands of Christ Jesus the Messiah," said dad.

CHAPTER 10

BLUE AND ZIBA ON THE RUN

Ziba and Blue are now on the run from authorities in Iran being aided by their friend Pete who used a set of keys he stole from the guards to free them while the earthquake and lightning were raining down on the land. They had a good head start and a secure hiding place awaiting nightfall before they can make their move again.

While they were in hiding Pete laid down the plan he said, "Our only chance to safety is to get to the Turkish border and cross it into Turkey. We cannot drive or appear anywhere in public because they will be looking for us everywhere." "Then what chances do we have?" asked Blue. "You see those mountains in front of us we are going to cross them on foot. I know the way and I have a lot of contacts on the route so prepare yourself to travel by night and rest during the day," said Pete. "I don't want you guys to worry about me I am in fairly good condition at the moment," said Ziba. Blue was happy to hear that so he hugged her and said, "When will we start moving Pete?" "In another two hours when its dark enough so sit down and get some rest," said Pete. Blue sat on the ground with his leg stretched out and Ziba sat beside him and put her head on his shoulder and they relaxed.

It was now night fall and before they began their long journey ahead Blue said a word of prayer asking for Christ Jesus the Messiah to guide, give them strength and protect them along the way. When they started their journey they tried their best not to even do any talking so they could reserve as much energy as possible because the route was steep in some places. They walked on and on sometimes in single file with Pete leading the way with his flash light and Ziba in the middle. They walked for about eight hours nonstop when they saw the sun starting to peep over the mountains in the east when they came upon a cave. "We will rest here during the day," said Pete. Those words could not have come at a better time for Ziba and Blue so they rested. "I have a piece of bread and a small tin of corned beef in my sack which we will eat now and drink some water," said Pete. "You thought of everything didn't you?" asked Blue. "Remember this is not my first journey through these mountains so I know what is required" said Pete. "Pete what do you call this part of the mountain?" asked Ziba who have never been here. "I'm not sure but tomorrow when we stop again we will be with some of my friends so I can ask them," said Pete. This time they needed a better rest than yesterday so Blue lie on the ground and Ziba lie beside him and put her head on his shoulder while they slept.

It was night fall again so they began their long journey ahead just like the night before when Pete shining his flash light said, "We are now deep into the mountains keep focused because we might encounter wild animals."

"Ok," said Blue who knew he had the responsibility of protecting Ziba with his life. They walked on and on for about nine hours till they saw the sun starting to peep over the mountains again but Pete did not stop because his friends were just a few minutes away. Even though the walking was much longer than the night before it wasn't as hectic because as they got deeper into the mountains the night temperature was much cooler. About thirty minutes after they reached the village where Pete friends were and what a jubilation it was when they saw him. "Who are these people?" asked Pete's friends. "This is Blue and this is Ziba," said Pete. "I know you just come from a long walk come let me show you where you can freshen up and rest while we prepare some food," said Pete's friend. They showed them to a hut which was reserved for visitors. It was beside a river fall so there they can take a bath. They did that, ate and rested.

Later that said day Blue, Ziba and Pete met with the elders of the village who gave them a brief history of the village. "Welcome to our village," said the chief elder. "We are most grateful to be here," said Blue and Ziba. "Pete your friend is one of us his mother and wife were born here and as you know not everyone is going to stay here but we are all sworn to secrecy that the outside world must never know about us," said the chief elder. "The people here are warm and loving the type of life Christ Jesus the Messiah taught about in the Holy Bible," said Blue. "Thank you for those kind words. We are all descendants of the twelve tribes of Israel, some of our ancestors came here thousands of years ago when they were scattered by the wrath of God and we have been here ever since. As you go along you will notice that all of us are fluent in the Hebrew language," said the chief elder. "How have you kept this place a secret after so many years?" asked Ziba. "We are surrounded by the dangerous valley of serpents which is feared by the outside world so no one would dare to come here," said the chief elder. "So how did Pete get in?" asked Blue. "Pete comes here time and time again so he knows the route quite well. We survive here because Christ the Messiah taught our ancestors about the power of the mind that it can move mountains and we have developed that mind control over the centuries" said the chief elder. "Wow that's amazing stuff, can you raise the dead like some of the apostles?" said Blue. "We have never tried that and we don't need to because people die here from old age. When you have a situation when your memory is fading, your sight and hearing are going and your joints are aching from old age you welcome death as a relief so your spirit can move on to its heavenly home," said the chief elder. "What is the average age of death here and how do you know that you have developed the power of the mind?" asked Ziba. "The average age of death is over one hundred years old and the power of the mind can only be exercised when the heart is clean and you have faith in God," said the chief elder. "That's why when my father died my mother packed up in England and returned to Iran because she wanted to be near to her roots and be contented," said Pete. "That's right because if you notice we do not have monetary wealth here but what we have here is worth more than gold. I want you to relax and enjoy our hospitality because tomorrow I'm going to take you through the valley of deadly serpents to the border," said the chief elder. "Thank you," said Blue who hugged Ziba and walked out of the hut not having a clue what the valley of serpents would be like.

During the night Ziba and Blue sat on a rock hugged each other and enjoyed the stars and moon light. They made future plans because they were confident that they were going to get home safely and the main one was to get married the same day if it's possible when they reached home. Ziba who was in total agreement with getting married the same day said, "Yes because we almost sinned twice forgetting that God sees everything and right this minute you are going to promise me that you will behave yourself when we are alone together." "Ziba It's not my intention to sin when I'm alone with you I will try to behave myself," said Blue. "Try! Didn't you see the wrath of God on display you really want to disobey him," said a very stern Ziba who knows that deep in her heart she is vulnerable to Blue's magic touch. Blue smiled and said, "Ziba I totally agree with you because God have been very good to us and we have a lot to be thankful for, I will behave myself I promise you that" said Blue. Ziba hugged him tight and said, "Thanks this is one of the reasons why I love you so much because you're very understanding, just a little more patience and I'll be all yours." Blue after hearing Ziba firm voice for the very first time now knows that he has to keep his promise looked at her and asked, "Ziba, do you love children?" "Most certainly" answered Ziba. "How many children would you like to have?" said Blue. "Good question I was wondering how you didn't ask something important like that before because husbands usually love to know that his wife will give him what he wants. Blue I will have any amount of children that you want but please be considerate because the type of profession that you have you will hardly be at home," said Ziba. "If the first two children is a boy and girl then I'm Ok with that but if the first two is of the same sex then I will definitely consider a third child," said Blue. "Then we have a deal and we will name them both together you and I will give them one name each," said Ziba who gave him a kiss on his cheek. Both of them sat there for about fifteen minutes not saying anything when Blue broke the silence and said, "I still have another two months before I start working because I requested three months from my prospective employers and I've only used up one so far to be here." "Oh that's wonderful we'll have lots of fun together during the remaining period without having to worry about incidents," said Ziba. "Sure I would definitely love to spend part of our honeymoon on the North Coast of Jamaica where we will have lots of Jamaican food and bask in the warm sunlight on Negril's white sand Beach." "Blue that sounds like heaven I can hardly wait to get there as husband and wife because I've never been on a white sand beach or had any Jamaican food before," said Ziba. They were so relaxed that they hardly said anything more to each other, all they knew was once they were in each other arms no words could compare with the moment they share. Blue prayed and gave God thanks then they retired to bed.

CHAPTER 11

GOING THROUGH THE VALLEY OF DEADLY SERPENTS

The next morning Blue and Ziba arose to the rising sun lighting up the village and when they went outside the hut they saw Pete waiting with some food he said, "Good morning, eat up my friends this is the last meal you will eat in Iran because later you should be in Turkey." "Those are some of the sweetest words I've heard since alighting from the plane some days ago. Pete went on to say, "My friends I want you to know that while you were in jail we had your back the entire way, we were waiting patiently for the right moment to break you out of jail. The armed guards were many so putting the plan into practice there might have been bloodshed but don't worry we were willing to risk it. The intervention of God saved the day and we are most grateful." "Thanks man you're a true Hebrew brother," said Blue. "It's our pleasure it's not the first time we had to pick up arms to fight against injustice but God had always stepped in to fight our battles," said Pete. "Pete, Ziba and I are asking you one more important favor to get a copy of her birth certificate from her mom and send it to us in Canada by whatever means necessary because some official form of identification is required when you are getting married in the West," said Blue. "I am not certain but I think I might be able to find one on one of my emails when I get to a computer with internet," said Ziba. "Good so we have everything all sorted out," said Blue. They ate and about one hour after they finished eating the chief elder was ready for the journey. Only four of them will set out on the journey, Blue, Ziba, Pete and the chief elder. Blue turned to the people in the village hugged some of them and said, "I will never forget you my friends and if God should spare life I think one day I might return here with my kids, goodbye my friends." There were tears of joy on their parting.

The real journey had just begun and about four hours walking when it was mid-day the chief elder stopped and showed them the mountain across the valley and said, "That mountain you see over there is Turkey, that's where you are going but first you must pass through the valley of deadly serpents. We will get there in one hour." They continued walking and when they reached the mouth of the valley of serpents they saw poisonous snakes crawling around everywhere. On seeing the serpents it made chills run up Blue and Ziba spine but their minds were made up that whatever is to be done will have to be done. The chief elder said, "Let's hold hands while I seek divine intervention for the next step of our journey." The chief elder prayed for about ten minutes and when he was done he gave his instructions, "Get into single file behind me, avoid eye contact with any snake, look straight ahead like what Peter should have done when Christ the Messiah told him to walk on the water towards him and do not show fear, have faith!" They started the journey through the serpents with snakes hissing as close as one foot away, some standing tall or hanging from trees as if they want to strike but faith in God and the power of the mind held them at bay and about forty minutes after they were clear of danger. When the chief elder said, "You can relax now we are through and safe." Blue stood speechless while Ziba broke down in tears and had to be consoled in his arms trying to come to grips with what she just experienced. "It's Ok to cry because you just completed the most terrifying walk in your entire life I don't think you'll ever face anything worse than that again," said the chief elder. Pete sat down beside Blue and Ziba because his filled stomach was suddenly feeling very empty. "Come let's keep moving because you have to be in Turkey before night fall," said the chief elder.

They continued the journey and when they reached the edge of the mountain there was a rope stretching from the edge of the mountain they were on in Iran to the mountain on the other side in Turkey. The chief elder showed them a rolling wheel and said, "We have only one rolling wheel so both of you have to travel together because when it goes over it's not going to come back because of the angle. The distance is about four hundred feet so Blue you will have to show great grit and strength in carrying both of you. Look straight ahead and focus let your love take you through because this is the last hurrah." They were starting to get signals from their friends on the other side so the chief elder looked at them and said, "It's time."

Ziba and Blue hugged a worried looking Pete and said, "Thanks! You have my phone number, my email address this cannot be our last meeting you can come to Canada anytime you wish remember you have an English birth certificate so it shouldn't be difficult and as an airline pilot I can get discounted airline tickets. Thanks Chief Elder." "Come hurry because if soldiers are in the valley and see you they are going to shoot at you. Keep quiet and don't panic just keep going," said the chief elder. Ziba lapped her legs around Blue hugged him tight and off they went rolling across the valley at full speed. Pete could hardly look and when they reached half way machine guns were fired at them by the soldiers patrolling the valley below but they kept going safely until they reached. When the chief elder was satisfied that they were safe he said to Pete who was worrying about his friends, "Come let's start our journey back and don't worry about the soldiers because they cannot come further than where they are." "I'm not worried about the soldiers chief elder I can deal with them, I'm just concerned that two of the most likable friends I've ever had I might not see them again," said Pete. "You're so right with that because when they sleep and wake they will not have any memory of the village and the valley of serpents but they will remember everything else. The only way they will remember anything about the village and valley of serpents they must have Hebrew blood in them," said the chief elder. "I'm not so sure about Blue because looking at Western black history there's a possibility that he might have Hebrew blood in him," said Pete.

The contacts on the other side quickly loaded them into a waiting van and sped away from the area trying to avoid confrontation. The two contacts in the vehicle introduced themselves as Ameer and Aryo to Blue and Ziba. Ameer told Blue and Ziba that he was Pete's uncle so they should relax because they were in good hands and they were finally in Turkey. Blue told the two gentlemen thanks and noticed that they were strapped with their 9mm Browning semi-automatic pistols. Ziba said, "Blue we've made it God has answered our prayers." It was a big difference from Iran they saw some women without scarfs and heard music playing on some streets. They were driven straight to the Canadian Embassy where they met with the Canadian consulate. After telling the consulate everything they did a background check on Blue and saw that he is a Canadian citizen. They could even tell that he was given a job offer to fly the national airline and also when he landed in Iran. Ziba was granted political asylum and they were given somewhere safe to stay until the paperwork was done.

While all that was going on Ziba's dad who had just gotten the news on the television of Ziba and Blue's escape decided to join the search party because he was determined that once they disrespect Prophet Mohammed there must be no hiding place for them. He knew most of Ziba's friends so he started checking them to find out if they had seen Ziba and Blue because they must be getting help from somewhere to be eluding Iran intelligence like that. But the guards who on duty when Blue and Ziba escaped were facing prosecution from their superiors because Blue and Ziba could not be found anywhere and the search was still continuing. Their explanation of Blue and Ziba's disappearance was not convincing to their superiors so their superiors branded them as cowards and irresponsible liars, the punishment if Blue and Ziba are not found was between five to ten years in prison.

Meanwhile in Canada by Blue's parent's house his mom and dad were sleeping because it was night in Canada when the phone rang and woke them up. "I wonder who it could be at this hour of the night disturbing us" said dad. He answered the phone yawning when he heard Blue voice on the other side of the line saying, "Hello dad it's me Blue" "Blue! Are you Ok?" said dad in a state of jubilation. When Blue's mom heard the loud shout of Blue she ran and put her ear to the phone also. "I can't talk long dad because I'm calling from Turkey and it's a long story. Ziba and I will be landing in Ontario, Canada tomorrow night at 9 o'clock please come and pick us up at the airport and tell mom hi for us," said Blue and hung up. Blue's dad after hanging up the phone said to his wife, "He did it, Blue actually did it, he took the love of his life out of his dreams and brought her into reality. When they come home we'll have to have a man to man talk because I'll really love to know how he did what some thought was the impossible, he's a true Simpson." "From the look of this we may soon be happy grandparents," said Blue's mom who suddenly didn't seem sick anymore. A few minutes after Blue's dad made about twenty phone calls that night telling everyone that he heard from Blue and he was Ok so prayers were answered and of course you know the type of celebration that will be planned.

The next morning after a good night's rest Blue and Ziba boarded an Air Canada plane which took off on time from Turkey with other passengers. While they were mid-way their long journey Blue said to Ziba, "I'm already missing Pete, the chief elder and the other people in the village but as for the valley of serpents that's a place I will never forget." "What village and valley of serpents are you talking about?" asked a surprise Ziba. "You don't remember those people and places that I just mentioned?" "No Blue I do not have a clue what you are talking about" said Ziba. Blue just smiled because when Pete contacts him he should know why Ziba is not remembering anything. They continued on their happy journey and when they land it will be on Canadian soil.

THE END